Female Nature

Jordan Henderson

Grosvenor House
Publishing Limited

This book is published by
Grosvenor House Publishing Ltd
Link House
140 The Broadway, Tolworth, Surrey, KT6 7HT.
www.grosvenorhousepublishing.co.uk

A CIP record for this book
is available from the British Library

ISBN 978-1-83975-979-6

Contents

Chapter 1: Introduction

Men and women are not the same. Men and women are opposites and opposites attract. However, western society has taught men that women are just the same as them, and that the only difference between men and women in the past were social constructs. This is a lie. Furthermore, there has been an enormous amount of propaganda by media outlets claiming that women are extremely complicated, and that you will never be able to understand them. Again, that is a lie. Women are actually very easy to understand, you were just never taught. Once you understand female nature and feminine energy, you will find it very easy to understand women. Not only that, but you will also find it a lot easier to understand the universe, which is mainly feminine energy. You will also increase your chances of experiencing success in life.

Whether you choose to deal with women or not, this book will benefit you because your interaction with feminine energy will determine much of how your life goes. Also, much of what will make you successful with women will also make you successful in life, the two are linked.

Chapter 2: What Is A Woman?

A woman is feminine energy in the physical form. Furthermore, a woman is the middle ground in between men and children. Essentially, a woman is the other half of the biological equation. Therefore, what a woman is attracted to is the opposite of what she is.

In order to create a baby, you need masculine energy in the physical form (male) and feminine energy in the physical form (female). Forget about all the technology you see around you today and see things in their basic biological form. Women are physically weaker than men and have to go through pregnancy; they are the dependent sex. Furthermore, the reproductive responsibility falls on women. As a result of this women must to be careful who they reproduce with and rely on. This is because as soon as a woman put her trust in you (with regards to survival), she would then (historically speaking) rely on you for food, safety, and shelter. Additionally, when she became pregnant for nine months, she would want to make sure you were one, capable of securing safety and security for her and her offspring, and two committed to her. That is why women like a guy who loves her but will stand up to her.

Due to technology and feminism women can now earn money, own property, and live without men (although they still need men for reproduction). However, our DNA does not know that it is 2021, which is why women are still attracted to the same thing. Women will claim they do not need a man and be on dating websites the very next week. This is because despite owning their own home, and making their own money, women are still biologically hardwired to seek out a man for provision and protection. Technology and feminism clashes with biology and has caused much confusion and dysfunction. It is almost like our subconscious does not register technology, but our conscious does.

Essentially, women are biological algorithms filtering for the best genetic material possible to reproduce with. Much of their behaviour can be seen as a filtering mechanism, filtering strong men and weak men by testing them. These tests quickly qualify the strong and disqualify the weak. The tests can seem trivial but can reveal strength and weaknesses. A few examples are when a woman tries to change a date time at the last minute to test your frame, or when she asks you to pass her an object that is closer to her, or when she insults you to test your core. These tests are done to separate the strong from the weak and are often carried out oblivious to most men.

Chapter 3: Male Nature vs Female Nature

www.youtube.com/jordanhenderson87
www.patreon.com/jordanhenderson (exclusive content)

To understand female nature, we must also briefly look at male nature. Men are productive, women are reproductive. Men are active, women are reactive. Think about the fact that in most cases a man actively pursues a woman, and the woman reacts to his energy, whether that is by approval or rejection.

Male nature is aggressive and dominating, it is about breaking boundaries, plus looking at what appears unrealistic, and then making it a reality. Examples could be inventing boats to travel across seas and oceans, inventing cars to travel over long distances in a shorter space of time, or inventing planes to travel even longer distances. Furthermore, men are equipped with testosterone which aids men's ability to carry out what is required. Much of male nature is about taking the lead.

On the other hand, female nature is much more passive. Women have more of a safety-first approach. This is due to the fact that they have weaker bodies, and because of childbearing. They are far less likely to care about leading, breaking boundaries, or taking risks.

Here is a list of comparisons between men and women,

Masculine	**Feminine**
Doing	Being
Rushing	Caring
Dominant	Submissive
Analytical	Intuitive
Striving	Tranquil
Busy	Calm

As you can see there are clear differences between male nature and female nature. This manifests itself in the physical world and you can see that through the behavioural differences displayed by men and women. Men are supposed to lead and are biologically equipped to do so with superior intelligence, mental, and physical strength.

Another point to add is that men are objective and women are subjective. Men see themselves in relation to the world, whereas women see the world in relation to themselves. Men are more capable of objective analysis while being emotionally removed from the subject matter, whereas women take everything personally. It is also very noticeable that women cannot handle criticism, rejection, or setbacks as well as men. One of the reasons for this is because part of being a man is going through suffering setbacks and being able to bounce back from them, therefore men need to be able to handle setbacks and criticism. Women are far more protected from the harsh realities of life than men and are consequently less equipped to deal with setbacks and criticism. Another reason is because men are far more capable of self-improvement than women. Thus, if a man is criticized or suffers a setback, he is far more mentally equipped to learn from the situation, improve, and prevent the same situation occurring again. Women cannot do this as effectively as men, and therefore are more prone to repeating the same mistakes over, and over again. They lack the ability to improve and as a result they will not take criticism well or handle setbacks well.

Chapter 4: Women Love Differently

When you say, 'I love you' and a woman says, 'I love you', it means two different things. Men love inwardly and women love outwardly. Remember that opposites attract. You were probably made to believe that women are just the same as you and therefore assumed that they love in the same way. That is not the case.

A man loves a woman's being and loves her for her. Whereas a woman loves what a man can do for her. She loves how you can make her **feel**. If you are able to make a woman feel excitement, safety, and uncertainty, she will like you. If you can make her laugh and feel good in bed, she will want you around. The minute you stop making her feel good is when her attraction towards you will start to decrease, and that is when things will start to go wrong in your relationship.

A woman may love you for the lifestyle that you are able to provide as this gives her the feeling of safety and security. Providing resources is fulfilling part of her nesting instincts and as a result makes her feel safe. Therefore, she will like how that feels, but the danger and thrill is what gets her wet.

If you are a man who is only good at providing resources and you are short, fat, and ugly, if at some point you can no longer provide those resources, and she stops associating you with safety and security, it is probably only a matter of time before she leaves you. She may very well of told you before that she loves you but will still leave you if you can no longer provide the resources you once did. You might wonder to yourself, 'how can a woman say that she loves me and leave because I'm struggling financially?' It is because she loved the feeling of safety and security which you no longer make her feel. **Women love differently to men.** You might also be reading this and thinking, 'how can a woman not love me for me?' or 'how can women be like this?' Women are not evil; the reason women behave like this is because of reproduction and survival. In the hunter gatherer days if a man could not provide resources, there was a high probability of death for her and her offspring. Therefore, the only option for her would be to find a new mate who could provide the resources that she needs.

If a man can make a woman feel good and provide resources this is an indication of strong genetic material, which is what women want. This is all driven by reproduction. Women are not evil, they have their reproductive function, and they love differently to men.

Chapter 5: Hypergamy

Hypergamy is the word used to describe the fact that women are always looking for better, even when they are with you.

You may think your relationship is going well but a woman is still going to be looking around. Women have a much smaller reproductive window than men, they have much less time to get it done, and they must find the best genetic material possible in that short space of time. A woman could have your children and live in a comfortable home but if a famous rapper came knocking on the door, she would at least think about it. This is an example of hypergamy.

Remember,

Hypergamy is not logical.
Hypergamy does not care about stability.
Hypergamy does not care about all you have done for her.

Learn these facts.

Now imagine you are a respectable 7/10 male. You are 35 years old, 5'10 inches tall, in decent shape, make 50k a year, and you have your own home. You also have some savings. You meet a 24-year-old woman who is from a poor family. She has got a pretty face but is slightly overweight, not well kept, and has a child from a previous relationship. The father never stuck around and does not financially support his child. Despite all that, you take her and her child on. You give her a home, a car to drive around in, and pay for her to go to the gym. A few years later you get married and you think things are going extremely well. Then five years down the line she starts acting off with you. You then subsequently find out that she cheated on you with a 20-year-old man. This 20-year-old still lives at home, makes no money, and is in and out of prison. However, he is taller than you and in better shape than you. To make things worse, after cheating on you this woman files for divorce and keeps the home. You are then told you must pay alimony and child support for another man's child.

The reason this woman cheated on you is because on a subconscious level she thought the 20-year-old has better genes than you. What about all you have done for her? Hypergamy does not care.

Hypergamy is not always accurate. That is why a woman may leave you for the better deal but come running back three months later because the man she left you for is not what she thought he was. This is because a man may seem appealing to a woman at first glance. Also, he may portray a certain image to get her in to bed and may even lie about certain parts of his life and circumstances. He may say he lives in a big house, drives a fancy car, and has lots of cash to impress a woman. However, he may be lying about part or all these things. Therefore, he may appear like a better deal than you but in reality, he is not. So, a woman may cheat on you or leave you for him, however when the woman realizes he is not what he made himself out to be, she may leave him, and come running back to you.

Women rarely leave a man without having another relationship to go to. Therefore, if a woman dumps you, she most likely has another man she is already seeing. It is common for women when they are thinking about leaving you to see what is out there and test the waters first. She may want to see what the new guy is all about before deciding to leave you for him. Also, a woman may use a beta male orbiter who she knows has wanted to get with her for an extremely long time. She may just use him for company so she can dump you and then find someone who she actually wants to be with later on. Back to the main point though, women will rarely just dump you and be single. Whether it is a relationship or someone she is just having casual sex with, she probably has something sorted out by the time she dumps you.

Here are some examples of hypergamous behaviour, the first one being girl's night out. Why does a woman in a relationship need to go to the bars and clubs? I am sure you all know the main reason for bars and clubs. Even though she is with you she wants to see how attractive she still is by the looks she gets in the bars and clubs. She also wants to see if there are any good prospects out there. Additionally, if she does get with a man on a night out, you best believe that you will be the last to know about it (if you ever even find out). Here is another question, why does a woman in a relationship need to wear makeup and dress in a sexual way out in public? They may say it is for them, but does she dress up to walk around the house? Does she go to bed with makeup on? If the shops were deserted, would she dress up and put makeup on knowing she will be the only person in the shopping centre?

A woman will not always act out on her hypergamous nature, especially if she is chasing a new partner, got a good thing going with her current partner, or does not think her chances of securing a new better partner are particularly high. For example, if she has a good thing going with you and she meets a man of similar value, maybe even of slighter higher value, however she is not sure it is worth the risk, she may not attempt to leave. However, be aware hypergamy is still there, and if certain circumstances present themselves, a woman may act on her hypergamous instincts.

Hypergamy applies to all men, low value men, average men, and high value men. Women even leave high value men because of hypergamy. You cannot stop hypergamy, you can suppress it by keeping her chasing you. After all, women do not leave men they are constantly having to chasing. Not only that, but you can also suppress it by maintaining a high level of attraction. However, the fact remains you cannot eliminate hypergamy. This is because it has been hardwired in to females to make sure they are always reproducing with the best males possible, which is beneficial for the survival of the species.

Hypergamy while good for the gene pool is not good for having stable societies. When hypergamy is allowed to run wild, a large number of women sleep with a small number of men. This is because all women want the top males. However, when this occurs most men miss out on reproductive opportunities. When hypergamy is controlled by social rules and laws which effectively discourage women from being hypergamous and leaving a man, this allows for stable families, which leads to stable societies.

Most men are average, anything from 4/10 to 7/10 is within the average range, so in for order a society to be stable and to function, the average man must be made to feel happy to some extent. Most men are happy with a woman who they know is not going anywhere, children, and stability. This happened in the past but is no longer guaranteed because hypergamy is now being allowed to run wild. To add that, society is built on compromise, everyone compromises for the benefit of the collective. However, the people in that society must feel they are being adequately compensated for their compromise and contribution. Men's compromise is not spreading seed to as many women as possible, which is men's biological mating strategy. Also, most men will labour in jobs they may or may not like for eight hours a day, five days a week. In past times the return for a man's compromises and contributions would be that they would get a woman, reproductive opportunities, and stability. Women would compromise by not acting out on their hypergamous nature and in return they get a man who is willing to labour for her and her children. When safety, security, and stability is established a society can experience advancement and progress.

Nowadays men no longer get the same benefits and are still expected to compromise and contribute. Men's benefits for participating in western society has decreased, while women's benefits in western society have increased. A man is still expected to sacrifice what he wants out of life to take on a woman and children. However, due to hypergamy running wild that family can be taken away from him at any time. This has led to groups such as Red Pill, Black Pill, MGTOW (Men Going Their Own Way), MRA (Men's Rights Activists), and Incels (Involuntarily Celibate).

It is also important to mention that female expectation never goes down. Once a woman has been with a man of a certain value, that is her expectation from that point onwards. So, say a 2/10 woman dates an 8/10 male, that is now her expectation. From the sex to the emotional stimulation, to the money, that is her expectation despite only being a 2/10 herself. Have you ever wondered why you see overweight women on dating apps saying things on their profile such as 'has to be 6 feet tall, in shape, and have his own place'? A woman may go for less because she cannot lock a high value male down in to a long-term relationship but she will resent him for the fact that she feels she deserves better.

Men did not need to know about all of this in the past to not get hurt because social rules and laws protected men. However, nowadays it is extremely important for men to learn this information to avoid unfortunate circumstances which can occur when a man is oblivious to female nature. All men should learn about female nature regardless of the time they are living in.

Chapter 6: Female Own Group Preference

www.youtube.com/jordanhenderson87
www.patreon.com/jordanhenderson (exclusive content)

Women will back women in conflict most of the time, whether the woman is in the right or in the wrong. This is called female own group preference.

Have you ever been in a situation where you are in the right and the woman is in the wrong, yet the women take her side, and show her support? For example, a woman cheats on you but the narrative is you were not paying her enough attention. You were always at work trying to provide, or you never listened to her. Therefore, her dropping her knickers and letting another man inside her is apparently your fault. This is then enforced by her social circles and now the narrative is that you are in the wrong. This is an example of female own group preference. Additionally, notice how often men will also take a woman's side over yours. This is because of men's weakness for women. **Women stand up for women, men stand up for women, hardly anyone stands up for men**. Remember that. The reason for this is because in the hunter gather days while male members of the tribe were hunting and doing other tasks necessary for survival, the women stayed at home, socialized with other women in the tribe, and looked after the children.

They cooked, cleaned, and looked after the children together. As a result of this, women formed a different type of social relationship towards each other than men.

Men's relationships were based more on working together to achieve a common objective and was essentially goal based. Examples of men working together to achieve a common goal and objective were hunting wild animals, fighting off enemy tribes, and building homes. Women's relationships were based more on keeping each other company and belonging to a social circle. With men for the most part, if you got the job done you belonged, whereas with women it was based more on fitting in to a social group. Due to the harsher conditions back then, coupled with women being the physically weaker sex, women did not want to be ostracized from the group, because that could mean death for her and her offspring. So, women sharing that interest stuck together and if they could blame something on a man then they would. Only in extreme circumstances would the women turn on another woman. Men would also blame another man, if possible, because of men's overall weakness for women. Also, if a woman is still in the group, then she presents a potential mating opportunity.

I am going to end this chapter by telling you that as a man you will get blamed and possibly even socially ostracized if you get in to an argument with a woman, whether you are in the right or wrong. Women avoid agency and shame at all costs. They will make up all sorts of lies about you that are not even remotely true to avoid taking responsibility for their actions.

Chapter 7: Lack Of Agency

Some of what I mentioned in the last chapter is relevant here. Women have a lack of agency and avoid taking responsibility for their actions. Women will lie, deflect, and run away from responsibility.

You might say to a woman, 'can you stop sitting on the couch in your bare feet?' and she might say, 'well you always forget to put your plate in the sink.' What she has effectively done is deflected the topic of conversation by changing the subject and trying to blame you for something else. The point is for that moment in time, whether you always forget to put your plate in the sink is irrelevant because you are talking about something she is doing. However, she has tried to deflect by blaming you for something else. Women do this a lot, and it is due to a lack of agency.

As I previously mentioned, women will turn the collective against a man if it means securing the safety of her position in the collective. This is because women were less able to survive on their own back in the hunter gatherer days. Ostracization from the group back then could mean death for her and her offspring. Remember, if it comes down to it, most women will lie if it means avoiding ostracization from the collective.

Women always want it to be your fault. Even when she wants you to approach her and she likes you, she still wants it to be your fault. What I mean by that is when a woman likes the look of you for example in a night club, she may move close within your proximity, bump in to you, or make eye contact. However, a lot of the time she still wants you to approach her and start the conversation; she still wants it to be your fault. Even a date that ends up with you and her having sex, a woman wants you to make all the plans. She just wants to go with the flow and if you have sex she can say 'it just happened'. She wants it to be your fault. You invited her back to your place, so it is your fault, even though she wanted to have sex as well. She needs an excuse, and the excuse is you invited her back to yours and it 'just happened'. That way she does not look like a loose woman in front of her friends. Her getting you to make the first move and starting the conversation also puts her in an advantageous position. This is because if you approach her and she changes her mind and is no longer feeling it, she can reject you, even though she encouraged you to talk to her in the first place. She can also tell people it was you who approached her even though she encouraged it.

A woman wants you to make all the decisions in a relationship because if it goes wrong, then it is your fault. If you let a woman make the decisions, you best believe she may still find a way to make it your fault if something goes wrong.

Women's lack of agency is because of a fear of ostracization from the group. Women will avoid, deflect, and deny in order to avoid taking responsibility for their actions. A woman may apologize for her actions, but this is only if there is a perceived benefit in doing so. For example, you have a lot of money and she cheated on you. She then proceeds to apologize and tries to keep the relationship going. Although she did indeed apologize, this is not the same as her genuinely being sorry and taking responsibility. She simply does not want to lose the benefits of being with you.

Again, women will generally avoid taking responsibility for their actions. **It is always a man's fault**. Because of this, women lack the ability to improve themselves in the same way that a man can. They do not want to be held accountable and men will often protect women from accountability as well. Now, you might think that men being held accountable, and women not being held accountable is a bad thing, but as matter of fact it is a good thing. By taking responsibility for your actions and taking the consequences you can fully learn from your mistakes and improve. Responsibility and agency are often pushed on to men, whether it is a man's fault or not. Many men in the west today have taken on feminine traits, and one of them is avoidance of blame. If you observe around you today, you will notice that many men have a lack of agency. When something goes wrong, it is almost like a competition of who can avoid responsibility. My advice is that if something is your fault, then take responsibility for it. This allows you to improve and grow as a person. It is sometimes hard to admit that you were at fault but sometimes to grow as a person you must admit it was your fault and take full responsibility. Do not deny yourself the opportunity to improve, take agency for your actions.

Chapter 8: Attraction

The universe is full of different energies vibrating at different frequencies. To add to that, the universe must keep replicating, renewing, and expanding, otherwise it will crash. For replication to occur, two opposing energies must be attracted to one another, this creates the best conditions for replication. This happens all the time in the universe. **Opposites attract**. Think about magnets, when you put a blue and red magnet together, they attract and come together. When you put a blue and blue magnet together, they repel. The same will occur if you put a red and red magnet together, they will repel. This is the universe showing you that this is an incompatible combination. When you have a '+' which is masculine energy and a '−' which is feminine energy, this is a compatible combination for replication to occur.

Your eyes are merely a perception of the universe. When you are in a body you can experience the universe in more of a physical manner. However, what we all are is different energies and we all vibrate at different frequencies. This impacts the way we interact and perceive the universe.

With regards to attraction, if men and women are different energies which attract to make children, it would make sense that what men and women perceive as suitable for reproduction is different. Men will look for feminine traits and women will look for masculine traits, and this is genetically hardwired in to us. How else will a man know what to look for in a woman? And how else will a woman know what to look for in a man?

Examples of what men look for are,

- Good looks.
- Good figure.
- Youth.
- No previous sexual partners.
- Passive personality.
- Good with children.

Examples of what women look for are,

- Confidence.
- Leadership skills.
- Resources.
- Social status.
- Not a pushover.
- Physical strength.
- Other women want you.
- Purpose and drive.
- Good at sex.
- Maturity.
- Funny.
- Good looks.

As you can see, men and women are opposites, and opposites attract. What men and women both look for is different. Attraction would not work if both sexes were the same and looked for the same thing.

Remember, for replication to occur opposites must attract. In the west today, women are being told to be like men, and as a consequence women have now become more masculine. Women have moved away from their feminine and have become less compatible. As a result they are now less of an opposite and are having less children. Reproduction is a form of replication; the equation is male and female equals child. The female has now become more like the male, and this has disrupted compatibility. Now each woman is having less children as a result. Women have also become less attractive now that they are more masculine, and this has manifested itself in their behaviour. They now clash with men instead of working with men, they now sleep around like men, and they are now in the workplace like men.

Have you also noticed that men have become more feminine? Women are being told to be loud and bold while at the same time men are being told to be sensitive and emotional. This has caused confusion between the sexes. I believe that men have become more feminine because of social conditioning but also as a subconscious response to try and rebalance the reproductive equation.

Opposites attract. The more masculine you are and the more feminine she is, the more different you are going to be. Here is an example of a difference between male and female attraction. We all know that women like a guy with money but when is the last time you got turned on by a woman's job? Men do not care about a woman's job because it means nothing with regards to her looks and fertility. Women do care about a man's job because it is directed related to his ability to provide and protect her and her offspring.

Chapter 9: Women Are More Selfish

www.youtube.com/jordanhenderson87
www.patreon.com/jordanhenderson (exclusive content)

Women are naturally more selfish than men and there are multiple reasons for this. Women see children as an extension of themselves. So, if a woman see's her child as an extension of herself, they have to be more selfish. This helps to keep the species going. To further my point, look at how vulnerable children are until they get older. When the males are busy providing and children are left in the care of the mother, the mother must be prepared to fight if necessary. You fight harder for what you love.

In nature the weaker organisms must be more selfish. Think about children, look at how vulnerable they are and look at what they need. Examples of what they need are food, water, shelter, and sleep. Secondly unlike men and women, children need many things delivered directly to them. To add to that, they also need protection from the physical world. Does your four-year-old son really appreciate all that you do for him? Of course not, if anything he probably **expects it**, and if there is any disruption to the norm he will probably complain. This is because children are more selfish. It is only when we are older, we look at what our parents did and truly appreciate it.

Whilst women are not as weak as children, they still have weaker bodies than men and need more protection than men. Furthermore, they are more vulnerable during the pregnancy period. Also, remember women see children as an extension of themselves. Women are more selfish than men and you can see this in their behaviour. When a woman is in a bad mood, she expects you to handle her throwing a strop, however if you throw that same strop, she will have a problem with it. What about when she makes you wait two hours before showing up to a date? However, on the other hand, if you are ten minutes late to a date, she gives you the silent treatment.

Men are expected to provide and protect plus they are expected to put women and children first. For much of history this is exactly what men have done, whether it be fighting in wars to protect their country from invaders, saving women and children first in moments of danger, or even simply going to work to provide for their family. Men have put women and children first throughout history.

Chapter 10: Why Women Love A Bad Boy

Women are told from a young age that they are the prize and that men should chase them. By the time they are in their twenties the average woman gets messages from multiple guys wanting to get her number. She gets calls, texts, and approached by guys out in public. The end goal for these guys is to have sex. Most guys chase women, the bad boy makes her chase him.

Most men are upfront, thirsty, and boring with women. They tell a woman who he is, what he does and how beautiful she is. He takes her on expensive dates before he really knows her. He then proceeds to buys her gifts and starts talking about relationships. This takes away the challenge. Bad boys on the other hand, do not take her out on expensive dates, they do not buy her gifts, or bring up being in a relationship. Unlike most men the bad boy takes his time to reply to her messages. He may ignore her calls, or he may turn up three hours late to a date. Instead of being upfront and keen, the bad boy acts indifferent and distant. This presents women with a challenge, which women love. The bad boy may act really in to her at times and then all of a sudden pull away. Women want to work him out. A woman does not need to work a nice guy out because he has already shown her everything about himself.

Imagine a woman has been told from a young age how men should chase her and that she is the prize, and for the most part this is backed up by men chasing her. Then comes along a man who does the complete opposite. He ignores her calls, he ignores her texts, and he shows up late to dates. This will play on a woman's mind. It will make her think, 'is there something wrong with me?', 'He is different' or, 'Why isn't he chasing me?' He is also being mysterious. Then suddenly all societal norms go out the window. This man may still live at home, be in and out of prison, or he may have no money. She does not care, she will call him, text him, and try to meet him at one o'clock in the morning. He is a mystery and a challenge. She will turn down men who have stable careers, their own place, and come from stable families. You could tell her every reason why you think she should be with you; it will not matter.

Bad boys communicate high value. Furthermore, bad boys play hard to get, and it is a universal concept that something harder to get is of higher value. For example, when you are playing on the Playstation, you feel better when you finally win against the boss after previously losing eight times because of the challenge. On the other hand, you do not feel a great sense of achievement when you beat the rubbish fighter on level one, because it was too easy.

Women tend to chase bad boys until around their late twenties to early mid-thirties. After that many women will then settle down with a safe dependable guy. Some women will say they have 'had their fun.' However, the truth for many women is that they were either unsuccessful in locking a bad boy in to a long-term commitment, or they wasted their peak fertility years having casual flings. The safe dependable guy thinks he is winning; however, he is not. He is getting the bad boy's leftovers. Even worse he is getting her when she is in her late twenties to early mid-thirties, when she is older and less fertile. At this stage she will also probably have more emotional baggage and resentment towards men. To add to that, you must pay for her expenses such as housing her, clothing her, and feeding her. You must also listen to her nagging and her emotional outbursts. The bad boy never had to do all that, he most likely just had sex and left the next morning. He just had casual sex; however, you have now got to provide for her, protect her, and marry her. Even then you and her may hardly have sex. A nice guy may think he is winning when he gets a woman in her late twenties to early mid-thirties, but often he is not.

Chapter 11: Forget Logic
When Talking To Women

When women talk to you, they want to **feel** something. Women are not logical creatures, logic does not work with women, save it for your friends. Men are logical and because people think men and women are the same, they and try and talk to women like they are men. Your job is to make her aroused, make her laugh, and be mysterious. This will increase your success with women. Because western society has told women to look for certain traits in a guy, that is what women **will say** they are in to or what they are looking for in a man, but it is not. They will say they want a guy who is honest, up front, and treats her like an equal, however this is not the case. Always look at woman's actions and not her words, the two are often very different.

If a woman asks you what you do for a living, you certainly do not ask her what she does for a living. That does not get her aroused, make her laugh, nor is it mysterious. The subject of work is often a logical conversation. Do not treat her like a man, forget what the west says, she wants to be treated like a woman.

Never give direct answers to a woman's questions. For example, a woman may say, 'what are you up to?' You could say, 'a few bits and pieces.' Most men would say,

'I'm walking the dog, going to the supermarket, then I'm meeting some friends.' If she asks, 'do you eat Caribbean food?' you could say, 'depends' instead of, 'that's my favourite.' If she asks, 'what's your favourite sport?' you could say, 'there's a few I like actually' instead of saying, 'football.'

Do not be so upfront with women, present a challenge. Most men think speaking to women as if they are men is how you should speak to women, and it is not. You will annoy her, bore her, and make her pull away from you, if you talk to her like she is one of your guy friends.

Chapter 12: Tests

www.youtube.com/jordanhenderson87
www.patreon.com/jordanhenderson (exclusive content)

As I briefly discussed in chapter two, women test men all the time, and most men are oblivious to it. These are mate selection strategies because of natural selection. The tests are testing how high value a man is.

Let us have a look at some of the tests that women give men.

You and a woman are eating pizza and there is some ketchup. She asks you to pass her the ketchup even though it is closer to her or the same distance away. Now, most men would not think twice and just pass her the ketchup. Some men may even think that passing her the ketchup will increase his chances of attracting her, if he is trying to pursue her. However, what you are showing her by passing her the ketchup is that you see her as higher value than you, and women do not find this attractive. That is how a servant behaves. A high value male will politely but firmly tell her to get it herself. You might think this will make her think you are a jerk, however this will actually increase her attraction towards you.

Now let us say you have arranged to meet a woman on Friday night. You arranged it last week but then on Thursday night she messages you and asks, 'can we meet Saturday afternoon instead? I've got to clean the house.' Now a lot of men will say, 'that's fine' and just agree to meet on Saturday afternoon. However, what you need to understand is that women will often try to change plans at the last minute to test your frame. A high value male is always busy because he is focusing on his goals. He cannot just change his plans at the last minute because a woman asks him to. Do you think a man with a big business can just change plans at the last minute? On the other hand, a low value male with no goals who only wants to please women will change his plans to whatever day a woman says. This communicates low value and if he agrees to change to Saturday afternoon, do not be surprised if she cancels on that as well. Whereas, if you politely but firmly say, 'this is the time we've agreed to meet, I'm free on this day, if not we'll have to meet another time', what you have done is held your frame (which women find very attractive), and do not be surprised if the woman goes back on herself and says she will meet you on the original date.

Another test is letting a man have sex on condition. I have heard of a woman who said to her partner he cannot have sex with her if he grows a beard. This is using the man's desire to have sex with her against him and testing his core. A low value male will comply and stay clean shaven, whereas a high value male with options will grow the beard regardless because that is something he wants to do. Furthermore, a high value male knows he can get with someone else if she is unhappy with his beard. He also knows that if she will not have sex with him, another woman will. It is also likely that if a man grows his beard when she tells him not to, she will end up having sex with him, even though she said she would not. Staying clean shaven will decrease attraction, growing the beard will increase attraction.

The reason women test men is because if a man cannot even stand up to a woman and is a pushover, this subconsciously suggests that he will also go out in to the world, and be a pushover when competing with other men. This may result in him bringing back less resources for her and her offspring. Going back to where the woman changes the meeting date, women like a man who makes decisive, definitive plans, and is sure of himself. This is because if a woman puts her trust in you, she wants you to be sure of yourself. If a threatening situation occurs, she needs you to be sure of yourself. Another reason a woman wants you to be sure of yourself is because women are indecisive by nature. Women always second guess themselves, change their minds, and lack direction. Therefore, what women look for in a man is someone who is decisive, someone who is sure of himself, and someone who knows what direction he is going in life.

The tests may seem petty but there is a biological reason behind them. Passing tests will increase attraction. Western society tells you to be a nice guy, however nice guys finish last. A lot of what I am saying will go against what you want to do but you will become more attractive to women if you do it. If you pass a woman's tests attraction will increase, if you fail a woman's tests attraction will decrease. The more a woman likes you the less she will test you, the less she likes you the more she will test you. If she likes you a lot, you can make more mistakes.

The tests never stop in a relationship. A woman will constantly test you to make sure you are good enough for her, so you cannot get complacent. She will still test you even if you have been together for ten, twenty, or thirty years. Learn how to stand your ground with women when it is necessary to do so.

Chapter 13: Marriage

Marriage is a contract between a man, a woman, and the government, and the government is on the woman's side. A marriage is the only license you do not need to pass a test for. If you want, you can have a woman, have children, and live together without getting married. If you get married you risk half your belongings, not to mention you will possibly have to pay child support and alimony. You are essentially paying her not to be with you. Marriage is extremely risky for men. Please consider that 50% of marriages fail and 80% of divorces are initiated by women. Out of the 50% of marriages that do not end up in divorce, how many of those marriages are happy marriages? Also, some of that 50% is people who got married yesterday.

A divorce can cause extremely hard times for a man. Child support, alimony, and losing half your belongings are just a few examples. Then having to pay for solicitors who charge £200 an hour and are incentivized to purposely drag out the divorce to profit from the misfortune of a failed marriage. The emotional side of a failed marriage can also cause a man much distress. Losing someone you love, no longer seeing your children everyday, or losing your home that you worked so hard to pay for. Is it really worth the risk just so you can have the big day? If you really want to you can live with a woman, have children, and live as a family without getting married. Even then you must be careful because if you live in a place that has common law marriage, then your split could be seen as that of a married couple (common law marriage is when you live together for a certain amount of time you can still be considered married in certain locations).

Marriage benefits women far more than it benefits men. Not to mention the fact that women are mainly the ones who push for marriage, and women are the ones who are doing most of the divorcing. Marriage is like relationship insurance to women. They get benefits when they are with you and benefits when they are not with you. They have incentives to divorce. You might think you have got a great relationship and your girlfriend might even say with regards to divorce, 'it won't happen to us', but I am sure many people said that. A woman may not even get married with the intention of divorcing you but if the relationship starts to go through a rough patch, instead of toughing it out like women did in the 1950s, all her friends will tell her the benefits of divorcing. They will talk about how they kept the house, car, and custody of the children. They will also talk about how they were able to hook up with a younger guy (who ended up using her before trading up) and how they receive monthly payments from their ex-husbands. On top of that, western society will tell her on TV, magazines, and the internet to be a strong independent woman, and how she 'don't need no man.' All of this results in a woman leaving you when in past times she would have stayed.

A woman has no incentive to behave in a marriage. She does not have to be passive, polite, or warm. She will see no reason not to go on girl's nights out. She may see no reason to have sex with you. On the other hand, if you do not go along with her demands, go where she tells you to go, buy her what she wants you to buy, or behave how she wants you to behave, she can divorce you. She will be backed by her social circles, backed by your social circles (who would have been narrowed down to who she approves of), backed by the government, and backed by western society as a whole. Also, do not think you can avoid the harsh reality of divorce by getting a prenup because a lot of them get thrown out of court.

I am going to end this chapter by asking you a question. What can you get out of a marriage that you cannot get unmarried?

Chapter 14: Male Disposability

'He's starting on me, sort him out!' 'Women and children on the lifeboats first!' 'There's a war, men to the frontline, your country needs you!'

Men are seen as the disposable sex and always have been. In past times men dying in wars was common, however on many occasions the women and children were spared. The women presented mating opportunities for the conquers and the children could either become future soldiers (male) or present future mating opportunities (female). This is a reason women become less attached to men than men become attached to women. Women had to get used to changing from one partner to another quickly, as this would increase chances of survival for her and her offspring.

Today men do not receive the same sympathy for depression, divorce, or being victims of violence. Women also receive lesser sentences for the same crime in some cases. If a male has sex with a legally underage girl he is seen as a monster, whereas if a female has sex with a legally underage boy, some will see it as 'lucky him'. Men are expected to risk their lives for women and children in moments of danger. If a man runs off in a moment of danger, he is shamed and called a coward. If a woman runs off in a moment of danger, it is seen as, 'she was just scared' or, 'she's just a woman.'

None of this seems like equality to me (equality is a biological impossibility anyway).

I want to draw your attention to the fact that despite more women working than in past times, the number of women working in dangerous jobs has not increased all that much. When it comes to jobs such as construction, you will hardly see any women standing high up on a half-built building, helping to put the building together. When it comes to policework, if there is a huge physical altercation to sort out, you are not going to see 20 women and 2 men going in to diffuse the altercation. It is far more likely you are going to see 20 men and 2 women going in to diffuse the situation. Finally, when it comes to heavy lifting jobs, you will hardly see any women in those roles. To the contrary, if a woman is working in a job such as customer service, and it temporarily becomes necessary to do some heavy lifting, for example lifting delivery boxes, you will often find women shying away from the role and asking a man to do it for her.

Women claim that they can do everything that a man can do yet they shy away from the dangerous jobs that men perform.

Men are seen as disposable utilities by women, governments, and corporations. It is time you realized you are **not** a utility. You are a soul in a human body, and you are unique.

Chapter 15: Women Are Like Children

www.youtube.com/jordanhenderson87
www.patreon.com/jordanhenderson (exclusive content)

Women are the middle ground in between men and children. As a result of this they have childlike behaviour. This is so they can relate to children.

Remember the mood swing or the silent treatment your thirty-five-year-old girlfriend gave you? Do you also remember the silent treatment your four-year-old gave you? Women are childlike and when you talk to them you must keep the conversation light. Generally speaking, women do not enjoy deep analytical conversations. Remember what I said before, women want to feel something. Save the deep analytical conversations for your friends. When you are talking to women keep it light, funny, and not too serious. Women are immature.

There are many childlike behaviours carried out by women that are either brushed off or forgotten about. However, these same behaviours are simply not tolerated when it comes to men. Here are some examples of behaviours that are seen as acceptable for women to carry out but not men.

When a woman has an emotional outburst, people just accept it, some people may even try to appease her. The emotional outburst could be over something trivial; however, people will rush to the woman's aid to make sure she is okay. On the other hand, if a man has an emotional outburst, a lot less people will be concerned about making sure that he is okay. People will often be of the opinion that a man should just be quiet, get it on with it, and sort out his own problems. Furthermore, many people will either lose respect for a man who has an emotional outburst, or even mock him. This is because people will see a man showing emotional vulnerability as a sign of weakness. Thus, a woman having an emotional outburst, comparable to that of a child is seen as acceptable, whereas a man having an emotional outburst comparable to that of a child, is not seen as acceptable.

Another example of childlike behaviour that is seen as acceptable when displayed by women but not men is one that I have already briefly discussed early in this chapter, and that is silent treatment. When a woman feels that you have upset her and she decides to ignore you right to your face, this is seen as acceptable. People will say, 'you've obviously really upset her', or, 'you need to fix what you're doing wrong', or, 'you need to apologize for what you have done.' You will rarely hear people say, 'she's being extremely immature.' If you were to give a woman silent treatment, you would receive criticism from the woman in question, the woman's friends, and possibly even your own friends as well. You would be labelled 'childish' and told to fix up.

When a woman laughs at a man and mocks him this is far more tolerated than when a man laughs at a woman and mocks her. If a woman mocks a man, she may be backed by woman and even men. Whereas if a man were to mock a woman, people would see him as horrible and criticize him.

Knowing that women are childlike, you should also not take the mood swings, silent treatment, and immature behaviour personally. Just take it for what it is, let her get it out of her system, and tell her you will discuss her issue when she has calmed down. Do not put up with violence from a woman, if a woman keeps getting violent, leave.

Chapter 16: Success In Life vs Success With Women

Much of what is takes to be successful with women will also help you achieve success in life.

To be successful with women you must be confident. Being confident also helps you achieve success in life. For example, if you are confident in a job interview, that will increase your chances of getting the job.

Women respect a guy who is not a pushover. If you are not a pushover in life, you will be respected by men, women, and children.

If you are patient women will like that about you as it demonstrates you are not desperate. If you are patient in life, your opportunity may come along when you least expect it.

If you are persistent, you will improve your success with women. If you are persistent at a particular craft, you will improve over time.

Women like a guy with leadership qualities. If you have leadership qualities in life, people will look up to you, and look to you for direction.

If you have money women will never be too far away. If you have money people will associate you with success and want to be around you.

Often women will not stick around during difficult times but will be around for the good times. In life, many people only want to know you when things are going well.

If you are selfish women will be attracted towards you. Selfish people often put their goals and ambitions before others, which helps them achieve their goals.

Women are attracted to a man who is prepared to go against social norms for what he believes in. People who go against social norms sometimes end up being leaders and pillars of strength. These men can also invent or discover, both of which can lead to improving people's lives.

As you can see there is a direct link between success with women and success in life. This is because the universe is mainly feminine energy. It is worth noting that if you want success in life, you will probably have to sacrifice women now and have them later.

Chapter 17: It's A Numbers Game

If Ronaldo approached 1000 women in the street, at least one woman would say no. Women are a numbers game. You can increase your chances by improving yourself (for yourself not women) but there are still no guarantees.

One day you could approach 10 women and get 8 numbers. The next day you could approach 10 women and get 5 numbers. The day after that you could approach 10 women and get 7 numbers. The numbers you get are a combination of your sexual market value, the environment, the mood the women you approached were in, and more. You cannot control everything, but you can increase your chances by being the best version of yourself.

A low value male has a lower chance of attracting women, a high value male has a higher chance of attracting women, but nothing is guaranteed.

Chapter 18: Success

www.youtube.com/jordanhenderson87
www.patreon.com/jordanhenderson (exclusive content)

You will increase your chances of success by increasing your energy frequency vibration. Always be the best you can be and never stop trying to improve. This will increase your chances of success, but nothing is guaranteed. Circumstances, environment, and timing can impact your success. One may know how to achieve something but because of external factors may not be able to achieve it.

We are all biological competitors fighting over finite resources. In the biological fight over finite resources someone has got to lose, and it is your job to make sure that it is not you.

Find fulfillment outside of payment, this will help you to be happy. Passion as occupation can destroy the passion (but not always).

In your journey, knowing when to strike is crucial, knowing when to rest is essential, and not comparing yourself to others is key.

No two stories are exactly the same.

If your family and friends do not support you but strangers do, keep going. Often family and friends are the last on board.

A boxer who is European Champion may want to become World Champion, however there is a queue of other fighters who want to fight the current World Champion. Therefore, the European Champion must wait.

What the European Champion does in between now and when he becomes World Champion, may be more important than what he does when he is the World Champion. Does he stay disciplined with his training and eating? Does he deal with the frustration of waiting? Does he make smart decisions while waiting for his fight? If he is told he will get to fight the World Champion in one year, as long as he does not lose in that time, does he fight a boxer with a good chance of beating him, or does he fight a tune-up fight which is less risky?

If you are climbing a mountain and you are 2nd place, you do not give a rope to 4th place, or they might climb up to 2nd place and push you down to 4th.

Opportunities do not always go to the most talented. I have seen boxers in the gym better than ones on television. A musician may have all the talent, but an opportunity may go to the musician with less talent because he walked to the shops while singing his song at the right time. Do not wait for an opportunity to come your way, it evades the desperate. Create your own opportunity by being creative. You do not need fame, just happiness, independence, and freedom.

Fame may or may not come, anyone who's only aim is to become famous is likely of questionable character. Opportunities often go to those who already have their own thing going on and may not even need the opportunity.

Corporations can pick people off the street who are not the most talented and the next day they will be famous. The people who are seen to be better than others are not necessarily better, and in some cases are most definitely not. In a natural state of survival, it is much harder to fake superiority. Things are not in order right now so do not focus so much on where others see you. Are you happy? Are you doing what you want to do? Are you surviving?

A lot of famous people want you to focus on what they eat for breakfast at 8:31, what coat they wear while they sit on the toilet, and what sunglasses they wear in the winter. None of this helps you achieve anything. If you ever become famous, **be different**.

Positive energy is the best energy. The universe has a habit of reflecting your energy back to you.

Do not drive your money, wear your money, or get high with your money. If the Gucci t-shirt you have on costs more than the amount of money you have, it is time to re-evaluate. The expensive car should be pocket money to the person driving it.

If you are not achieving your goals, then you need to re-think your strategy. For example, you want to make a living as a musician, and it is not working out. Look at what is working out or what else you are good at. Make a lot of money doing that and use that money to help with music. Money used correctly can help you.

Energy impacts energy so surround yourself with positive people and avoid negative people. People talk a good game but when you are losing no one seems to care. If you find a rare person who does, remember him, and treat him well.

Say minimal to a gossip, your business to him is like a big plate of food to a starving man.

Chapter 19: The Female Chameleon

When a woman decides that she likes you, she will often try to mimic your interests, and pretend to be in to the same things that you are in to. This is despite the fact she may have no interest in what you are in to at all. For example, you may be in to Rugby. You start talking to a woman and she eventually develops feelings for you. Now your new girlfriend starts going to Rugby games, starts sending you Rugby videos from YouTube, and starts talking about Rugby a lot. It is not that she has all of a sudden developed an interest in Rugby, it is because she likes you, and she knows that you are in to Rugby. Therefore, by pretending to be in to Rugby herself, she is trying to appeal to you in the hope that you will develop stronger feelings for her.

If you and the woman you are seeing breakup with each other and she starts seeing somebody else, she may go from being a Rugby expert, to being a Tennis expert within a week. This is because she is trying to appeal to her new partner.

Chapter 20: Virgins Are Better

Women have been told they can sleep around like men, and it is the same. It is not the same at all.

Women suffer far more emotional damage by sleeping around than men. Their dopamine and oxytocin levels drop with each new sexual partner. This decreases their ability to bond with you. Also, once a woman has been with many men, she will always compare you to them, and you will always be competing with her past sexual partners. She can be with you while thinking about someone else. This will increase the chances of her getting bored of you and looking elsewhere. Furthermore, women retain the sperm of their past sexual partners, and it stays within their body for life. When you have sex with a woman you leave an impression on her.

Virgins are not damaged and are far more likely to follow your lead than women who have been with many men. A woman who has had a lot of past sexual partners is not a good choice. She has slept with 20 guys, had no expectations of those men, but you are supposed to provide and protect for her? Past behaviour is a prediction for future behaviour, remember that.

A woman will often settle for a nice guy after having casual sex all throughout her twenties. She spent her best years having casual sex with bad boys and now she expects the nice guy to forget about her past and provide for her.

A man who has slept around with lots of different women is attractive to other women because he has experience. Women think, 'if all these women want him, then I want him too.' Women may also think, 'if he has been with all those women, he must be doing something right.' This is because a man who has had many sexual encounters with lots of different women is communicating that he has strong genetic material. Additionally, men do not suffer the same damage by sleeping around that women do. A high value male will not want a relationship with a woman who has slept with lots of different men over a woman who is a virgin.

Chapter 21: Dating Is Dangerous

www.youtube.com/jordanhenderson87
www.patreon.com/jordanhenderson (exclusive content)

Some women will not tell you that they have STDs. This can obviously have severe consequences on your sexual health and your overall health in general. In some cases, women with STDs feel like they either have no obligation to tell you that they have STDs, or they feel angry at the fact that they caught those STDs in the first place. They then take that anger out on other men by sleeping with them without letting them know that they have STDs. There have been cases where women with HIV have slept with men, knowing full well they have HIV. Furthermore, men have caught HIV off women because the woman did not tell the man they have HIV. Those men now have no choice but to live with a disease that will most likely end up killing them. This makes these women extremely dangerous, so you need to be careful. A lot of young men in particular think with their penis and not with their brain. So, you need to ask yourself this question, is taking a risk for a one-night stand worth having a disease for the rest of your life?

False rape accusations can ruin your reputation, whether you are found innocent or guilty. If you have been wrongly convicted of rape, do you think prisoners are going to care if you are innocent? You can expect to be a social outcast, picked on, and beaten up by other prisoners. Do not be surprised if even the prison guards facilitate situations where prisoners are able to beat you up. If you are wrongly convicted of rape, do not expect prison to be easy. Additionally, you will be forced to sign on to a sexual offender's register. This will lead to people you do not even know being able to look you up, and they will identify you as a sexual offender. Most people will not question whether it is true or false, especially if it is a man who was convicted of committing sexual offences against a woman.

A further impact of this will be future job opportunities. You will struggle to find work, even lower paying jobs such as working in a supermarket, waiting jobs, or being a cleaner. The minute a potential employer finds out that you have a conviction for a sexual offence, you will most likely be unsuccessful in your application. Even people with other offences such as robbery or assault may be considered for job roles before you. Plus, you can forget working with children or even a job where children are around, such as in a supermarket. Even worse, if you have children of your own, you could lose access to them.

You will more than likely be socially ostracized by your friends and maybe even your own family if you are wrongly convicted of a sexual offence. Some people just will not want to be associated with somebody who has been convicted of a sexual offence because of the impact it could have on their life. They will be worried about being associated with you because it may impact their job security, reputation amongst friends, or the relationship they have with their partner.

A false rape accusation can ruin your life.

A woman may get a used condom and try to get herself pregnant. Or she may poke holes in condoms in the hope that she can get pregnant. Becoming a father when you were not planning to can completely change the direction of your life. Any plans you had for the future such as starting a business, focusing on education, or travelling will most likely be greatly compromised if you become a father. Children are wonderful and I am not for one second saying becoming a parent is something you should not do. What I am saying is that if you become a parent when you were not planning to, it has the potential to change the direction of your life. Furthermore, if you become a parent and the mother is somebody who you did not plan to become a parent with, this can cause huge problems for you, and most importantly, the child.

If you date a woman who does not tell you she has a boyfriend, you could find yourself in a physical altercation over a woman. Remember, women will often test the waters with a new man before leaving their current partner. This has the potential to not end very well for you because if her current partner finds out that you are seeing his girlfriend, you can end up having a physical altercation. Secondly, even if her current partner does not find out that you were her are seeing each other while she is still with her current partner, if at some point in the future he finds out that you were seeing her while she was still with him, you could have a problem. Remember, you do not know who you are dealing with. You could be dealing with a man who has mental issues, a violent man, or a gangster.

If you are going to date understand that it is dangerous. Women are protected by the law far more than men and as stated before, agency is always pushed on to men. Not dating is a sensible option.

Chapter 22: Sexual Market Value

Your sexual market value (SMV) is your value in the sexual marketplace. For example, one male may be an 8/10 and another male could be a 4/10. Your sexual market value is determined by things such as your looks, personality, and financial status. By identifying your current sexual market value, you can work on improving it.

An 8/10 male may have his own place, be in shape, and make 200k a year. A 5/10 male may live in a small flat, not workout much, and make 30k a year. A 3/10 male may live at home, work a minimum wage job, and be out of shape. The higher your sexual market value, the more success you will experience with the opposite sex.

Women's sexual market value is based on different things. While men's sexual market value is based on things such as looks, personality, and financial status, a woman's sexual market value is based on things such as fertility, lack of sexual partners, and nurturing skills.

A 9/10 woman may have great looks, no sexual history, and be in her early twenties. A 5/10 woman may have average looks, 2 previous sexual partners, and be in her early thirties. A 2/10 woman may not be good looking, have 5 previous sexual partners, and be in her late thirties.

Men tend to date down, and women tend to date up. Men tend to get better with age, whereas women tend to get worse with age. Women's sexual market value is higher when they are most fertile. If a man works on himself, as he gets older, he will become more attractive to the opposite sex.

Here are six things that go towards a man's sexual market value,

1. Personality.
2. Confidence.
3. Social Status.
4. Resources.
5. Looks.
6. Height.

Here are three things that go towards a woman's sexual market value,

1. Looks.
2. Fertility.
3. Previous number of sexual partners (the less the better).

For the most part, women in their twenties will have far more options with the opposite gender than men in their twenties. However, at about age 30, men's sexual market value and women's sexual market value meets in the middle. After that point, men start to have a better sexual market value than women their age. As a man's sexual market value increases, a woman's sexual market value decreases.

This is a sexual market value predictor and can vary,

Male SMV.	Female SMV.
20-23 – 2/10	17-19 – 9/10
24/26 – 3/10	20-24 – 10/10
27-29 – 4/10	25-26 – 9/10
30-32 – 5/10	27-28 – 8/10
33-37 – 6/10	29 – 7/10
38-42 – 7/10	30-32 – 6/10
43-45 – 8/10	33-35 – 5/10
46-48 – 9/10	36-38 – 4/10
49-55 – 10/10	39-41 – 3/10

As you can see, women's sexual market value decreases over time, whereas men's sexual market value increases over time. It is crucial for a woman to lock a man in to a long-term commitment while her sexual market value is high enough to compete with other women. However, feminism tells women that they can sleep around, have a career, and have a family. This is delusional because by the time a woman has been travelling, had a career, and slept around, she is going to be past her prime. Consequently, the men who are willing to give her commitment will be of lower value. A woman 35+ will not have the same options as 20-year-old women. A smart woman will lock a man in while she is still young, as that is the age that she will be able to attract a higher value male, compared to the type of men she will attract if she waits until she is older.

On the other hand, a higher value male in his forties who has worked on himself can attract much younger women, such as twenty-year-old women. He is in his prime with regards to personality, social status, and resources. Furthermore, if he has looked after himself, he may have retained his looks. She is in her prime looks and fertility wise, so it makes sense. He has experience, is more mature, and probably has more resources than most 20-year-old men. The woman is capable of giving him children and she still has her best eggs. They are both in their prime with regards to their sexual market value. Western society shames men who like younger women and you will hear things such as, 'get with a woman your own age.' This is to shame men who are capable of attracting younger, more fertile women, and instead getting them to settle down with an older woman, with a low sexual market value.

Chapter 23: Equality Is A Lie

From the moment sperm race to get to the egg, there is no equality.

When you take tests at school and are put in sets according to your ability, you are in competition. When you wrestle in the school playground while the girls watch to see who wins, you are in competition. When you go to your job interview and sit in the waiting room with the other candidates, you are in competition.

Nature thrives on competition to ensure the strongest form of the species survives. If the strongest form of a species is not surviving, this can lead to extinction. Do you watch a boxing fight to see if it is going to be a draw? No, you watch to see who is going to win. Women talk about equality, so why do they always gravitate towards the top males? Women like men with abs, who are good in bed, and have money. If you are fat, terrible in bed, and have no money, women will run away from you.

What about equal opportunities you may ask? And to that I would say, how does a child from a poor background have the same equal opportunities as a child from a rich background? What about the law you may ask, does the law not treat people equally? No, not at all. People with more money can afford better lawyers, which can help them negotiate shorter sentences, or beat a case that a poor person may not be able to beat. Additionally, rich people who generate more income and more tax for the government may get more leniency than a poorer person with a low income.

There is no equality. Believing in equality will decrease your drive. We are not all equal. Some people are physically stronger than others, some are more intelligent than others. These are the harsh facts, instead of believing in delusion, identify your strengths and maximize them. Corporations and governments benefit from you believing in equality and having a decreased drive. They do not want people walking around with lots of drive and ambition. They need someone to work in checkouts, call centers, or the reception desk.

Men and women are not equal. The chain of strength goes man, woman, child.

Men will fight each other over women. Much of many men's desire to be successful is to impress women. Many men will acquire money to impress women. Many men will acquire expensive clothes to impress women. And many men will drive expensive cars to impress women. To further my point, when you pursue women whether you realize it or not, you are competing with other men, even if you cannot physically see those other men.

Women will also fight each other over men. Women want to be as attractive as possible because of this. They know that most men are visual creatures and therefore the better they look, the more chance they have of attracting male attention.

The makeup, tight clothes, and expensive dresses are all an attempt to appear attractive to the opposite sex. Women know that the more visually attractive they are, the more male attention they shall receive.

Women will fight over men by trying to replace the girl he is currently with. Women want to appear virtuous but in reality, if a woman thinks that she has a good chance of taking a high value man away from another woman, the type of man who has got good looks, money, and social status, then many women will attempt to do so. This is not because women are horrible people, this is based on reproduction and survival. If a man has good looks, money, and social status, he is giving off signals that he has strong genetic material. Therefore, on a subconscious level a woman is going to think if she can be with that man, it increases her chance of securing safety and provision, plus it increases the chance of her having strong, healthy offspring. Going back to the point, women will fight each other over men, and are in competition with each other.

No matter how much the west tries to tell you that you are all equal, equality is a lie.

Chapter 24: Why Wasn't I Told About Female Nature?

www.patreon.com/jordanhenderson (exclusive content)

Society is built on male sacrifice; men are the backbone of society. Without men it all falls apart. Men fight in wars, build buildings, build train lines, work in sewers, invent, and take risks. Men give up their freedom to take on women and children. They will often work boring jobs to provide. Not only that but men are also shamed in to compliance. Men who do not date are seen as losers. You are told, 'you can't get laid', 'you hate women', or, 'who hurt you?' On the other hand, a woman who says she does not date and wants to be single is told she is 'strong', 'independent', or people say, 'you go girl, you don't need no man.' Men are shamed in to conformity. Society wants men married, working a full-time job, and not questioning anything.

If more men knew about female nature, then less men would be willing slaves on the plantation. When a man realizes women need him more than he needs them, women lose control over him. Big boobs, big bums, and pretty faces are cool but when a man becomes less controlled by his biology, he starts to focus on what he wants, and not what women want. When this happens, resource extraction becomes much more difficult.

Women are financially irresponsible. They like to buy excessive amounts of shoes, clothes, purses, and so on. Furthermore, go in to any shopping centre and you will notice that most of the marketing is aimed towards women. This is because corporations know women are bigger consumers than men. Women do 80% of the consuming and in that 20% that is not female consumption, how much of that spending is men purchasing for women?

For women to consume men must produce. Men do not need as much 'stuff' as women. If more men learned about female nature and opted out of society, refused to take women on, and refused to be wage slaves on the plantation, women would not be able to consume as much as they do today. Less money would then transfer from male to female. As a result of this, corporations would lose wage slaves in the form of men, and income revenue from the non-essentials that women spend money on. Also, governments would not be able to make as much money on tax. Society would fall apart. Plus, how many workplaces would survive without men? A society can function if only men work but can it function if only women work?

Women, governments, and corporations need men and shame men in to compliance. In the past men had more compensation for their sacrifice than they do today. In the past men had a woman who was not going anywhere, children, a stable job, and respect from his peers. Nowadays, men are seen as a joke and clueless buffoons (look at how men are portrayed on TV adverts). Not only that but most men are also expected to beg to go on a date that they are paying for. A woman is not guaranteed and if you do get one, she can divorce you, put you on child support, or both. If you say something that goes against the feminine imperative, you could also lose your job. Despite all of this, men are still expected to simp up, get married, work a full-time job, and take the risk. Well, many men are wising up. At some point in the future women may have a shortage of willing slaves to work on the plantation. Women say, 'I don't need no man', however I do not think that is true.

You have been kept in the dark about female nature to keep you in compliance. In recent years women, governments, and corporations have been so aggressive with the suppression and attack on masculinity that many men are now starting to take notice. Many men are now learning about female nature and how men are viewed by women, governments, and corporations.

Men who focus on themselves are much harder to be controlled by women, governments, and corporations. Men who are not easily controlled by a pretty face, big bums, and big boobs are harder to extract resources from by women. To add, men who are not married and are focused on their passions are harder to control by corporations. Corporations love a married man because he needs that job, or his wife will divorce him. He cannot just quit his job to focus on his goals or because he is being treated poorly. A married man is not going anywhere, will not rock the boat, and will be more likely to put up with being treated poorly. This is because he does not want to be divorced. He knows if he gets divorced, he can lose half his belongings, his home, be put on child support, and possibly be forced to pay alimony. A man who focuses on himself can live life on his own terms and spend his time on what he wants to spend his time on.

Chapter 25: Plausible Deniability

A technique that women often use is called plausible deniability. This is where they say something which you can neither prove nor disprove. For example, I could say, 'women are more irrational than men' and then a woman could say, 'well I know men who are more irrational than women.' Firstly, that is a weak argument because collectively speaking women are more irrational than men. Secondly, there are exceptions to every rule, so there are going to be men who are more irrational than women, but that is not the norm. And thirdly, she could be lying, however you can neither prove nor disprove what she is saying. This is an example of plausible deniability.

Women use this a lot as it helps them escape blame or defuse a valid point. A lot of men in that situation will cave in and maybe say, 'true some men are more irrational', instead of holding frame and saying, 'collectively speaking women are more irrational than men.'

Another example could be your girlfriend goes on a night out. The next day she receives a text from another guy she gave her number to when she was drunk. You question her about it, and she says that she was so drunk, the guy took her phone when she had it out, and put his number in. You can neither prove nor disprove what she is saying. This is plausible deniability.

Here is a third example of plausible deniability. You arrange a date with a woman and agree to meet at 20:00 outside a restaurant. You arrive at the restaurant at 19:50 and you wait for her to come. However, the woman suddenly stops replying to all your calls and all your text messages. You wait for two hours for her to come until you decide to go home because you realize she is not going to come. The next day the woman messages you, saying how sorry she is. She claims that she was running late, however she did drive past the restaurant at 20:30. She then explains how she did not see you standing outside, so she thought you must have just gone home, so she also went home.

The truth is she never even left the house that day and she certainly did not drive past the restaurant to see if you were there. However, unless you watched every single car that went past, the woman has plausible deniability. You cannot tell her that she did not drive past the restaurant to look for you because you did not watch every car that went past.

Chapter 26: Women Want You Irrational

When a man is thinking with his penis and not his brain, he is easier to control by women. However, when a man is thinking with his brain (which tends to happen as a man gets older) he is much harder to control.

Men who think with their penis are often taken advantage of by women and often act irrationally. He may buy a woman items that are not necessary such as shoes, clothes, and purses. He may take out a loan to get her an expensive car she does not need, or he may take her on an exotic vacation while he is struggling to pay the bills. The reason he is doing all this is for her validation, approval, and sex.

A man may also start to neglect his own interests and needs when he is acting irrationally. He may no longer find time for his hobbies or time to relax. Another situation that may occur is that he finds himself working so hard that he may not find the time to cook healthy meals, and because his woman refuses to cook, he starts getting fast food every day, and subsequently becomes unhealthy. Furthermore, a man may put himself in dangerous situations like physical confrontation with other men, or put himself in financial difficulty, all for a woman who once the man is no longer useful, will go and find someone else. Getting married just because your woman wants to without consideration for the number of failed marriages in the west is also an irrational choice for a man to make.

Women do not want you to think rationally when it comes to selecting a partner. This is because if you do think rationally when selecting a partner, this would exclude a large proportion of women immediately. If a man were to select his female partners rationally, this would immediately exclude women who have slept with many men, which is many women in the west today. It would also exclude women who are loud, argumentative, and rude, which again is many women in the west today. And it would also exclude single mothers, women with tattoos, feminists who hate men, and more. Women do not want you to consider a woman's past when deciding whether to be with her or not because again, this would exclude a lot of women immediately. Remember, past behaviour is an indication of future behaviour.

When a man is irrational, it makes him easier to be controlled by women. Additionally, it is easier for him to be used as an emotional tampon, to be used as a bodyguard, or to be used for resource extraction.

Chapter 27: Scarcity vs Abundance

www.youtube.com/jordanhenderson87
www.patreon.com/jordanhenderson (exclusive content)

Women want men who are chased by other women. Men want women who are chased by other men. If someone is in demand this communicates high value and strong genetic material. No woman wants the guy who cannot get laid. So, when you chase a woman non-stop, you are communicating to her that she is the only woman you can get, it is her or no one. No woman wants to feel like she is the only one you think you have a chance with. Therefore, if you chase a woman and communicate low value and scarcity, she will pull away from you. Men often think that if a woman pulls away, the best thing to do is to chase her to see what is wrong, so they can fix it. That is wrong. Women purposely test men by pulling away to see what he will do. If you show you are not bothered, attraction will increase. On the other hand, if you send her 35 messages asking where she is, or what is wrong, she will lose attraction towards you. By showing you are not bothered, you are showing her that you have other things to be getting on with. This is an indication of high value, strong genetic material, and abundance. Do you think a guy with 80 girls on his phone will care if one goes missing for a few days? Women want a guy with options.

This is also true away from women. If you have a smile on your face even when you are faced with hard times, people will wonder why that is and think you must be of some value.

The man who has an abundance of jobs offers can demand more money from the corporations offering him a role because if a corporation refuses, he can go to someone who will pay him what he wants. The man who only has one job offer and is in a position of scarcity cannot come with the same demands.

When times are tough a lot of people tend to walk around looking miserable, and this communicates low value. Furthermore, it communicates scarcity because people will subconsciously think, 'if he were more successful, he wouldn't be so miserable', which let me just add, is not always true.

Do not be fake but even when times are tough, try to remain positive with regards to self, and your interactions with others. It communicates an abundance of character. If you can remain positive even during hard times it says a lot about you as an individual. People will respect that about you and may even offer to help you out of a bad situation, whereas if you were projecting negative energy, they may not have.

People like people with options and people like people who are popular. The musician who can pull in a big crowd for a gig will be seen as more desirable than the musician who can only pull in a modest crowd. Ironically, the less popular musician out of the two may be a better musician, but unless he can pull in a bigger crowd, he will be seen as less desirable by others.

High school is a classic example to demonstrate that people like people who are popular. Every high school will have a popular crowd, everyone else, and the losers. Everyone wants to associate with the popular crowd. They want to be seen hanging out with the popular crowd, they want to sit with the popular crowd at lunchtime, and they want to be invited to the parties that the popular people go to. Most people would abandon their current friendship group to become part of the popular crowd. Sometimes, the people who are in the popular crowd turn out to be arrogant, rude, and shallow people. Furthermore, they may demonstrate more undesirable traits than other people who are not as popular. However, people will persist in their bid to gain approval of the popular crowd. This is because despite possibly showing undesirable characteristical traits, the people in the popular crowd are communicating through their social status, and popularity, high value, and abundance. They are getting all the girls, they are wearing all the cool clothes, and they are going to all the parties. The socially awkward geek may be kinder than the popular people, but no one wants to be his friend because girls do not desire him, he does not have cool clothes, and he never gets invited to parties.

Chapter 28: Social Conformity

Women are like a hive, they have more of a follower mentality than men. Even if they do not agree with something they will tend to go along with it if the majority are going along with it. To add to that, women will attempt to find out what is socially acceptable and try to make sure that everyone conforms to it. Additionally, women want familiarity as familiarity breeds comfort and safety. Shame and exclusion will be used to get men to conform. If there is a group of people hanging out together and a woman does not like what one of her boyfriend's friends is saying, she may tell her boyfriend he is not allowed to hang out with him. Most men will conform with what women want them to do because they want female validation, approval, and sex. Men who do not conform are labelled 'weird' and women will attempt to turn the collective against him.

The reason that women want everyone to conform to what is considered 'normal' is because of what I briefly mentioned earlier in this chapter. Women want comfort and safety, the reason for this is because comfort and safety are ideal grounds to raise and nurture offspring. If everyone has different ideas, opinions, and values, this can cause conflict, and potentially violence. Another reason women want people to conform to what is normal is because they are the physically weaker sex. Therefore, they are less able to defend themselves when a violent situation occurs. As a result of this women tend to be very risk averse and prefer environments where there is conformity and predictability.

As more women have entered the workplace, the workplace has become increasingly politically correct. In past times, men in the workplace were able to have arguments, be more aggressive, and talk in more of a freer manner than they are today. This was good because men could let things off their chest, have an argument there and then, and then get back to work. The workplace has become more feminine and politically correct due to the increased female presence in the workplace. The way men used to operate in the workplace in the past would make women feel uncomfortable if the workplace were to operate in such a way today. Consequently, men no longer say what they really want to say, they bottle up their emotions, and this is not a healthy environment for a man to operate in. If a man says what he wants to say in the workplace and is deemed to be politically incorrect, he can lose his job. This undoubtedly has had a negative impact on the mental state of men.

Chapter 29: Female Special Treatment

Women want equality and special treatment at the same time. They talk about how they are strong, independent, and do not need a man. Yet when it comes to dates, they still want a man to pay because that is what a 'gentleman' does. They say that they are strong but want a man to hold the door for them. Women will say 'ladies first' and talk about equality.

Whenever there is a war, it is certainly not 'ladies first' to the frontline in battle. If someone broke in to your house in the middle of the night, or you and your girlfriend got attacked in the middle of the street, it would not be 'ladies first'. Women have no problem with it being 'men first' when there is a perceived threat, but when it is safe, they want it to be 'ladies first.' This is hypocritical behaviour and goes against their whole invalid concept of equality.

Women want you to pay for the meal, pay for the drinks, and drop them home. Women want you to give them special treatment. However, when it suits them, they want to be treated the same as men.

Chapter 30: Women Lie More

www.youtube.com/jordanhenderson87
www.patreon.com/jordanhenderson (exclusive content)

Women lie more than men, even about small things. An example could be you ask a woman, 'did you clean the car?' She then says that she did when she in fact did not, even though it is a minor thing to lie about. Women will lie about the number of past sexual partners they have been with because they know on a subconscious level that it is wrong for a woman to have slept with many sexual partners. One sexual partner might mean three but the other two do not count because she was drunk.

Women lie about the fact that they are single when you start talking to them. Most women always have at least something going on, maybe even a relationship when you first start talking to them. Many women will test the waters with a new guy before leaving their current relationship. She may tell you that she is single when in reality she has a boyfriend and is testing the waters with you.

As well as lying about being single, women will also lie about their reasons for dumping you. Women rarely tell you the real reason they are dumping you. A woman may say, 'I'm not ready for a relationship.' When a woman says that to you, the question you need to be asking yourself is, if Justin Bieber came knocking on her door, do you think she would not be ready for a relationship? A woman may dump you and say, 'I need to find myself' or, 'it's not you, it's me' (which means it is you).

Another scenario is a woman may dump you because you are not good in bed, but she may tell you it is because she is going through a hard time. Women lie about their reasons for dumping you to avoid potentially violent repercussions, to appear kind, and so she can come back to you if she chooses.

In the hunter gatherer days when violence against women was more accepted, women feared violent repercussions from men. Consequently, women have developed the behavioural trait of preferring to lie or 'soften the blow', as opposed to telling a man the truth, when they fear the repercussions for doing so could result in violence.

Additionally, as I briefly mentioned earlier in this chapter, if a woman lies to you about why she is dumping you, she may be able to make the breakup more amicable. This means that if her new relationship does not work out, she has a better chance of being able to get back together with you if she feels that she wants to. Conclusively, by lying about the reason that she dumped you, a woman can increase her future options. Furthermore, a woman will appear kind to the collective by lying about her reasons for dumped you. An example could be a woman dumps you because you are not good in bed, and she does not find you attractive. However, she tells you, your family, and your friends that she is going through a stressful time because she is depressed, her home life is not good, and there is tension within her friendship group. The only people she tells the truth to are her best friends. This makes her reasons for dumping you seem much more acceptable to you, your family, and your friends. It may also make you and others sympathetic towards her. People will see this reason for dumping you far more socially acceptable than her telling people she dumped you because you are not good in bed, and she does not find you sexually attractive. Therefore, by lying, the woman in question maintains social acceptance (which is extremely important to women), and she is free to find someone who she finds sexually attractive, and who she feels is better in bed.

Women often lie about their reason for flopping on dates. Have you ever arranged to meet a woman, you are texting each other, it gets to an hour before you are supposed to meet, and silence? No calls, no texts, she just stops replying. You then call and text to see what is going on and you hear nothing. Then the next day you get a message from her saying how sorry she is and how her friend broke her arm. She then claims she had to driver her friend to the hospital, however her car broke down on the way there, and she feels so bad. That story is very unlikely. It is much more likely that for whatever reason she did not want to meet you. Women have a hard time telling a guy, 'I don't want to meet you', so they will just avoid the situation.

Women lie for many reasons, and they lie more than men. Always assume a woman is lying.

Chapter 31: Female Victim Mentality

Women always want to be the victims. Whenever a situation occurs, they are somehow always the victim. When you ask her about her past relationships, it is always the man's fault. When is the last time you heard a woman say about a past relationship, 'it was all my fault, that's why we're not together anymore'?

Women want to make out that men are horrible and have treated them poorly throughout history. The fact is that women have benefitted massively from men's technological and societal progress throughout history. From roads, to cars, to trains. From light bulbs, to telephones, to television, women have benefitted from the progress of men. Men invented technology and medication that reduces women's pain during childbirth, which was not a good idea. Furthermore, men have also given women forms of birth control which they are now using to sleep around, which again was not a good idea.

Men have also died in wars to protect women and children. Women say they are equal to men, well let me ask, how many women do you see fighting on the frontline during wars? They protest about how there needs to be more female CEOs, but you never hear how there should be more females working in sewers, building big buildings, or fighting on the frontline during wars.

The fact is that men have kept women alive and carried them throughout history, but you would not think that was the case with the attitude women have towards men today.

Remember, women always look to be the victims.

Chapter 32: Male Happiness

I have spoken about the biological fight over finite resources, how we are not all equal, and the truth about female nature. However, we are all going to die eventually so while we are here, we have got to try and be happy as much as possible. The information in this book should put you in a better position to make an informed choice about women and other areas in your life too. Hopefully, I can prevent men from making an uninformed and irrational choice that they later regret, and one that prevents them from being happy. Times are changing and you must adapt. You cannot pretend it is 1950 in 2022. What worked for your parents may or may not work for you.

Notice how in this book I never said, 'stay away from women.' I am not going to tell you that you must not date women, that is your choice. I am just telling you the truth. If women make you happy and you want to start a family and get married, you are your own man. Just understand that it is riskier than before. Also, it cannot be the number one priority in your life.

You cannot blame a woman for being a woman. Their nature is their nature and from a biological standpoint their nature has a purpose. What you need to do is learn about female nature and decide how you will navigate your way through your interactions with women.

Single or in a relationship I recommend you have a hobby that you commit to. If you speak to women, then your hobby must be something you do not stop because of a woman. For example, if your hobby is singing and you practice on Mondays and Thursdays, do not cancel your singing practice to go on dates.

A hobby will give you something to focus on outside of maybe work and family life. If work is stressing you out and you take two hours to focus on your hobby, during those two hours you will be thinking about your singing, basketball, or dancing, not those deadlines your boss has given you, the supervisor who is on your back, or the coworker you cannot stand. Your brain needs something unrelated to your family, bills, and work. You might say, 'I haven't got the time, I work 80 hours per week, and I have a family to take care of' or, 'I'm just too tired after my 80-hour work week.' You have time. Want to learn Spanish? Study 5 minutes per day, 10 minutes on a Saturday, and have Sunday off. How long does it take to learn to say 'hello' in Spanish, 5 minutes or 2 seconds? If you practice 5 minutes per day, 10 minutes on Saturday, and take Sunday off, that is roughly 140 hours per month. That is roughly 1680 minutes per year. How much Spanish can you learn in 1680 minutes? Quite a lot I would think. You can do that working 80 hours per week.

Paid or unpaid, have a hobby that you enjoy, and do not rely on to pay the bills.

A lot of men are unhappy right now and I want to help as many men as possible to be happy. I cannot tell you what will make you happy but what I can tell you is that you should try to be happy as much as you can. You should also be aware of the things that are a danger to your overall well-being.

I hope you have listened to what I have said about female nature. I also hope you understand that there is no equality. However, I also hope you understand you must find time for yourself in this crazy world. You must also make sure that you are happy.

Good luck.

CPSIA information can be obtained
at www.ICGtesting.com
Printed in the USA
LVHW100711010422
714940LV00006B/119

9 781839 759796